The Ministry to Persons with Disabilities

THE MINISTRY
TO PERSONS
WITH
DISABILITIES

Sister Jane Krafft, M.S.B.T.

THE LITURGICAL PRESS
Collegeville, Minnesota 56321

Cover design by Ann Blattner. Cover photo by Will and Angie Rumpf; used with permission.

Other photos courtesy of Sister Jane Krafft, M.S.B.T.; used with permission.

| 1 | 2 | 3 | 4 | 5 | 6 | 7 | 8 | 9 |

Contents

Preface

This booklet is written to help us in our ministry to our disabled neighbors—those with physical or mental impairments, whether temporary or chronic, who wish to be freely accepted as full-fledged members of the local community, the Church community, and the human community-at-large. Some will need but little help; others may need attendant care or full-time guidance and supervision. Our task as Christians is to determine what assistance is needed and offer whatever will allow each person to continue to grow and develop with dignity.

We are challenged to minister as Christ ministered: seeing beyond disability to ability; nurturing and challenging each person's abilities; and advocating in behalf of all of the disabled that they be allowed full access to an education, a job, medical and psychological counsel, and the sharing of God's blessings on our country.

> Sister Jane Krafft
> *Missionary Servants of the Most Blessed Trinity*

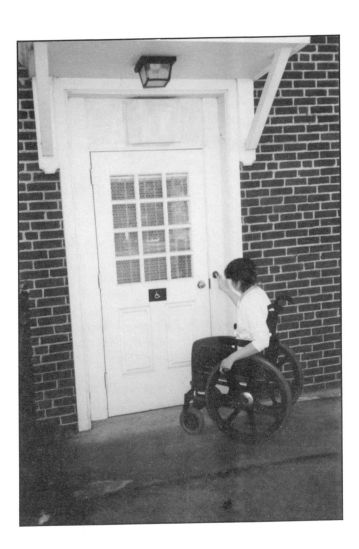

1

The Creation of a Nonperson—
a Case History

Mary, one of five children in a hardworking family, grew up in a small, rural mountain community in Appalachia. Barely able to eke out a living from the poor, worn-out soil, her father and brothers hired out to the local coal mine whenever there was work. They also tended a small tobacco patch, raised vegetables, and did occasional odd jobs. When the coal mine shut down for good, Mary's father commuted twenty miles to help out in an auto body shop. After years of living with the constant pressure of keeping his family together in a hand-to-mouth existence, Mary's father took to alcohol as a way of coping.

Mary was born with an abdominal tumor that would grow larger as she developed. Her parents viewed Mary's tumor as an affliction, a sign of God's displeasure with them, therefore a punishment. Consequently, no medical advice was ever sought, nor did her folks ever search for ways to make her life—the life of a developing person—as normal and comfortable as possible, given Mary's condition. What was worse, the family was ashamed of Mary, and Mary felt it bitterly.

Denied the medical attention she needed, Mary began the painful process of learning to survive with her handicap in a family environment that was ill-prepared to accept her. After all, Mary was different. There were countless times when she would remain at home while her brothers and sisters visited relatives and friends. There were seemingly endless arguments over why she had been born with a tumor and the shame the family attached to it. Mary wanted to lash out at them at these times, but little by little she retreated into the private world of the unwanted. It was easier that way. She felt like such a burden to everyone and began to feel a sense of guilt over her tumor, as though she, herself, were to blame for ever having come into the world that way. Her guilt seemed supported by the manner in which her family treated her.

In an effort to ease her guilt and inward hurt, Mary began to mask her feelings, regardless of what anyone said or did. As her father sought to cope by drinking more, Mary coped by becoming a non-person, just what they wanted her to be. She would never again ask a question or be assertive in any way. She would retreat to her room whenever an argument developed. She would shrink into her surroundings and be care-

---

Lord, help! Godly people are fast disappearing. Where in all the world can dependable ones be found?   —*Psalm 12:1*

---

ful not to intrude, lest she be blamed for creating even more disharmony. As a person, however unique and gifted she was, Mary had disappeared.

Mary's tumor grew so large that teachers who came to the house to help her felt uncomfortable. After a while they didn't come at all. Her parents never complained to the school authorities. One teacher had told her she couldn't read. Mary had decided, then, that she couldn't even be taught to read, and her parents went along with the idea. All throughout her grade-school years Mary drifted in imposed isolation—no trips anywhere, few visitors, no children to be friends with, no school ties, no playing house or dolls. What was it like to be somebody's friend? Mary was growing up ignorant of the kinds of childhood experiences that were common in America, even in her native Appalachia. She was a classic example of one who didn't know what she was missing.

As she grew into her teens, Mary was rarely let out of the sight of a family member, and she sensed keenly that lack of trust. She watched her brothers and sisters go to school, go on dates, learn to drive, and get married. Mary would not do these things. She was allowed only to watch others have fun. She was talked about but never to. Decisions were made for her, and she was expected to comply. She learned to deny her sexuality. After all, despite her attractiveness, Mary couldn't possibly consider a date with *her* disability! So she tried hard not to admit that she was female. But in truth, Mary was on the brink of becoming a young woman, and no one took the time to notice. This she would soon remedy. She would force others to notice her. Mary would become a person.

Mary's Breakthrough

At eighteen, Mary informed her parents that she wanted the tumor removed. They tried to talk her out of it, fearing for her life, the cost of it all, and suspicious of the medical system in general. Their fear for her life was well-grounded because the tumor was adjacent to her vital organs, and any attempt to remove it would be risky. Undaunted, Mary pursued the operation. She was suddenly determined to take control of her life and to suffer whatever consequences might come about. She had hope for herself, and she would undergo the risk to attain freedom from what she considered a life not worth living.

With the aid of a young doctor at a teaching hospital, Mary arranged for the financial assistance she would need. He told her that she would lose a leg in the operation and that the nature of the surgery would preclude her ever being fitted with an artificial one. Mary went ahead, knowing she would never walk again. She survived the extensive surgery, the months of therapy, and the yearlong stay in the hospital only to find that her parents had widened the gulf in their relationship by not being able to accept her "new" disability.

For a while, living back at home was the same dreary isolation that Mary had so long endured, only this time her "caretaker" family had to contend with her in a wheelchair. Things changed suddenly, however, when both of her parents died within a year of each other just before Mary's twenty-first birthday, a traumatic experience for this courageous daughter who from then on would daily ponder her parents'

In an ordered and productive community, it is a fundamental principle that every human being is a "person". . . [with] rights and duties . . . flowing from [one's] very nature. These rights are therefore universal, inviolable and inalienable.
—*Pacem in Terris*, encyclical letter of
Pope John XXIII

---

inability to understand her and to love her. "Was it all my fault?" she would ask. "Did I cause their deaths? Why wasn't I lovable?" In time, and with professional counseling, Mary would begin to understand, but not now.

Growing more accustomed to her wheelchair, Mary now took command. At a rehabilitation center she learned how to take care of herself and to develop vocational skills. She also gained some sorely needed self-confidence. She took up residence at an independent living unit, where she got a job working with senior citizens, an experience that gave her more confidence and the gradually increasing ability to love and be loved. From there Mary learned to drive, bought a car, and enrolled in college—a brave, young woman who had won for herself her own life.

Today, Mary is a well-regarded special education teacher who works with severely handicapped adults. She devotes her life to helping others in their journey to independence. She knows the dreams of those who are dependent on the care of others, the dreams of children who desperately want to live a childhood, the dreams of a teenager who wants to live life to the fullest. Those were Mary's dreams, and through sheer grit, determination to be her own person, and years of hard work, Mary turned those dreams into reality.

Have You Counted Your Blessings Lately?

Like the Mary of our case history, most people with a disability—congenital or acquired—find themselves in a world environment where there are normal expectations that everyone is the same. Persons who are not as mobile as others, or those who are immobile and need care, often live desperate lives of loneliness and self-loathing. Furthermore, they learn to apply the veneers of guilt, anger, and fear so that they may find excuses for not accommodating to the normal ebb and flow of life.

We might well ask how many Marys there are out there? How would I have reacted if I had been Mary? In other words, how many of us ponder our gifts: good health, the ability to work, to talk, to taste, to see and hear? All of us take these gifts for granted until one of them is taken from us by accident, illness, or misuse. We could lose our jobs! Our friends, maybe! Life, indeed, would be different. Sometimes, losing our

---

I give thanks to the Lord, for he is good; his loving kindness continues forever.   —*Psalm 136:1*

---

ability to take care of ourselves can be frightening, if not altogether devastating.

In counting your blessings consider this: Over 15% of the U.S. population has some kind of handicap. That translates into some 36 million people. Some of these handicaps are obvious: Down's Syndrome, blindness, people confined to wheelchairs. They get our attention immediately. It may take us longer to discern mental illness, deafness, problems of drug abuse and alcoholism, let alone the wide range of organic disorders that are not apparent to the eye.

No doubt many of us interact with our friends and colleagues on the job without being conscious of handicaps such as poor eyesight or speech impediments. Eyeglasses are so common that we don't even relate their use to the word handicap. And while we may not even notice whether friends are wearing corrective lenses to help them overcome a handicap, we certainly become quickly aware of someone with a disfiguring tumor like Mary's. Suddenly, it is difficult to deal with that particular man or woman as a *real person.*

Beyond Mary's problem are countless millions whose conditions cannot be altered by medical science. They are so severely disabled that they find themselves shunted from the mainstream of society. Once out of sight they tend to fall into the cracks and become nonpersons. These are the brain-damaged, the deformed, the paraplegics, the chronically disturbed. Jesus spoke about them many times. He took the time to listen to them and to have compassion for them. Can we have any less?

Jesus' Example

Jesus' example would have us overlook the handicap and focus instead on the inner person to see his or her wholeness. It is not an easy thing to do. Our struggle to be truly Christian and to accept as equals people who are different challenges us at all times. It is not always easy to reach out to men and women who are the objects of pity, people who are stared at or shunned by family and society-at-large. The right to life that Christians accept implies that whatever the physical quality of that life, every human must be given the opportunity to realize his or her full potential. This principle must apply to the most severely disabled as well as to the most gifted, physically normal person. And if we really believe that all life is sacred, then we must do as Jesus would have us do—in his name and for his love.

Read this booklet prayerfully. As you read, try to reach out in your heart to the Marys in your community. Let the words help to bring you an awareness of how to accept and assist those in your parish who struggle to be whole and wholly accepted. Do it within the framework of your faith community, because within that community there is a power-filled force that will allow us to bridge differences and accept each other as persons made in God's image and likeness.

Jesus heard the cries of his people, the afflicted, the poor, the outcast. He freely chose to live among them as a healer. He taught his followers to look deeper into people and to have compassion for whatever their plight. He lived out his words. We must take those words and go and do . . . just as he has done before us. We must take Jesus' command to minister seriously.

. . . the central meaning of Jesus' ministry is bound up with the fact that he sought the company of people who for one reason or another, were forced to live on the fringe of society. . . . The Church finds its true identity when it fully integrates itself with these "marginal people". . . .

—*Pastoral Statement on the Handicapped*

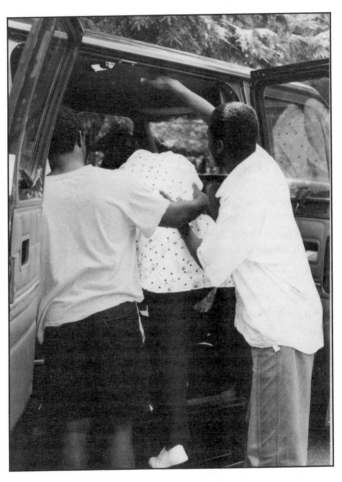

People helping people is what ministry is all about.

2

Treatment of the Disabled—
An Overview

Until a few years ago, a disabled person was often considered a shameful secret, someone who was hidden away by a family rather than being dealt with honestly. Such was the case with Mary's family that we saw in our first chapter. It is true that there will always be the backward family attitude like that of Mary's case, but for decades much the same attitude persisted generally throughout the country: keep them in the closet, so to speak. This "closet" attitude contributed largely to the policy of indifference, unofficial but real, in the United States until World War I.

With the return of fathers, brothers, and uncles from the terrible trench warfare in Europe, many of them limbless, blind, or emotionally ill, the national conscience seemed to awaken from its slumbering indifference. Gradually, we began to see these sick and disabled as real people. To meet the needs of returning veterans, scattered rehabilitation facilities and programs sprang up. Twenty-five years later, with millions of returning G.I.s from World War II, the nation began a concerted effort to make responsible improvements in care for the disabled.

In 1943, the government's Vocational Rehabilitation Act addressed itself primarily to the needs of disabled veterans, but it also recognized the needs of the mentally ill and the mentally handicapped. Eleven years later an amendment provided research and training programs to prepare professionals for work with the disabled. Another amendment, a decade later, provided for training and employment opportunities for the disabled in special community-based rehabilitation programs. Thus, it took almost forty-five years—1920–1965—to develop a national

---

> At the sight of the crowds, his heart was moved
> with pity. They were lying prostrate from exhaustion, like sheep without a shepherd . . .
>
> —*Matthew 9:36*

---

policy regarding the handicapped. Moreover, national policy aroused the Catholic Church leadership in the United States, and the Church set about to implement similar programs.

The Church had not been derelict in its duties to the disabled. In the 1800s religious orders of sisters had left their homelands to establish hospitals, schools, and social programs in the United States. They had administered to the disabled of the American Civil War at its bloody conclusion in 1865 and had continued to serve the veterans of both world wars.

Shortly after World War II, Catholic Charities of New York City involved itself in a cooperative networking venture with the Jewish Family Service, the Veterans Administration, and the Community Service Society to meet the needs of returning veterans. These agencies not only supplied their individual religious needs, but they also trained and supervised temporary housekeepers for such enterprises as the Bulova School for Watchmaking, which had been specifically established for paraplegic victims of the war. These private agencies offered individualized care in given neighborhoods and gradually introduced disabled veterans into community living and the workforce. The community-based programs were especially successful in helping veterans re-adapt to family living, and

> I will arise and defend the oppressed, the poor, the
> needy. I will rescue them as they have longed me
> to do.   —*Psalm 12:5*

local churches reached out, both clergy and laypeople, to assist agencies as psychologists and social workers.

Progress in the Sixties

The 1960s saw the first strong legislative commitments to the plight of the disabled: the right to an education, to have choices, the right to work, and the right to live a full, dignified life. The Kennedy years spearheaded interest especially in the mentally retarded. President John F. Kennedy's sister was retarded, and his entire family took the lead toward establishing the Special Olympics program that has helped so much to focus national attention on the needs of the mentally retarded. In fact, the nation's interest in the disabled, those mentally, physically, or emotionally handicapped, really came to the fore in the sixties.

It was during this period also that the movement toward community-based residential services developed, resulting primarily from the "deinstitutionalization" of state-run institutions. Up until the early 1960s, this country's response to virtually every person with a disability was to place him or her in a state institution, often committing them without the due

> I demand that you love each other as I have loved
> you.   —*John 15:12*

process of a court hearing. The deaf, the blind, the epileptic, the palsied, the retarded, and the mentally ill were "warehoused" in large, dehumanizing institutions. Accounts of living conditions in such places are the recitations of nightmares: people kept naked, rolling in excrement, kept in barren, chilly, locked wards. It was a national scandal that was finally redressed by a series of court cases that tested the constitutionality of committing people without the right of appeal. By the mid-seventies, almost every state had developed a plan to deinstitutionalize its large mental hospitals and developmental centers. These plans inevitably stressed the necessity for community-based services that included group homes, sheltered workshops, activity services, and day-care treatment centers.

Lord, when did we see you hungry and feed you,
or see you thirsty and give you drink?
—*Matthew 25:37*

Education and Employment

Close upon the heels of deinstitutionalization came the awareness that school systems had an obligation to provide education for children with disabilities. Public Law 94-142, passed in 1975, mandated public education for children from two to twenty-two and provided federal dollars to provide such service. This legislation guaranteed—for the first time—classroom access for all disabled children, regardless of what kind of handicap they might have. This law, with its subsequent amendments to provide the least restrictive school environment possible, resulted in thousands of disabled children being "mainstreamed" out of the family closet and into the public schools all over the country.

Civil rights laws and equal employment opportunities came next, along with the right of free access to public buildings, theaters, and the like. The wheelchair symbol is now commonplace in rest rooms, supermarkets, and federal and state office buildings, and it no longer seems strange to see disabled men and women in the workplace. America is becoming "normalized." Disabled and able-bodied alike are sharing responsibilities and rights in every town and city in the land.

3

From Legality to Reality

While the laws enacted over the past twenty years have made it illegal to discriminate in any way against the handicapped, completely free access to all avenues of American life has not necessarily followed. Words on paper are one thing, but what actually happens on a daily basis is another. In other words, all the legislation in the world will not change attitudes. For attitudes toward the disabled to change, each of us must look within ourselves to determine why we react in a certain way to a given situation.

A Self-Test

Test yourself. The following three stories are hypothetical but true-to-life. Read them and review them. Then try honestly to assess your emotional response. How would you react if involved in these situations?

The Jones Family. Mr. and Mrs. Jones just finished paying for the house they purchased thirty years ago. Theirs is a nice home in a neighborhood of older, but substantial, houses. As a result of the time, money, and care that they have put into the house, the place has appreciated tenfold in value, and the Joneses are justifiably proud of it. They plan to spend the rest of their lives there and leave it to their daughter when they die.

But last night their next-door neighbor dropped by to inform the Joneses that the house next door to her had been sold for the purpose of setting up a group home for the mentally retarded. The Joneses really didn't know anyone who was retarded, but the stereotype immediately came to mind: not very normal-looking people, somewhat strange and a little scary to watch—perhaps even dangerous! Who knows? And why are they moving into THIS neighborhood? The houses on the block won't be worth anything!

Now let's put ourselves in the Jones house. What was your reaction? Did you say to yourself, "I hope that never happens on our street!"? Did you think of property values, a dangerous element in the neighborhood—how do we fight this? Or did you think to yourself that this was going to be a great opportunity for our children to learn to realize that the mentally retarded can be warm and loving people, thus enriching their lives? Let's go over and welcome them when they move in! Perhaps.

Let's look at another case, the kind that happens every day:

The Personnel Manager. Jim Smith is responsible for interviewing engineers for a growing manufacturing company. He interviews candidates for each job opening and makes a final recommendation to his boss. Last week he narrowed down the field of candidates for a new position from twenty-five to five, each of whom would be excellent if given the job. One was exceptional: a *summa cum laude* graduate of a prestigious Ivy League school, with an excellent work record. He was personable and articulate—and in a wheelchair. His name was Hal.

During the interview Hal was candid about what he would require to accommodate his disability if he were given the job. The entrance to the plant would have to be ramped and the men's room door widened. Ramps would be needed in several other work areas as well as for access to the cafeteria. In short, hiring Hal was going to cost the company more than the usual relocation cost of bringing Hal and his family to the area. Jim Smith would have to think long and hard about this candidate before making his final recommendation. But Hal *was* the pick of the lot.

―――――――

If you were Jim Smith, what would be your decision? Would you have the courage to hire Hal and make the necessary changes in the physical plant so that you could get the best man? Could you honestly make a case for Hal with your supervisor so that he would see things your way?

Try another situation:

―――――――

The Washington School. At the last PTA meeting the parents learned that "mainstreaming" children from special education classes into the regular classroom situation was to begin next fall. When the parents asked just what kind of children they would be ("Would they be normal like the rest of the children?"), they were informed about different kinds of disabilities the children might bring with them: some would be mentally retarded, some emotionally disturbed, some blind or deaf, some with cerebral palsy or other physical problems that would require altering parts of the school building. When the parents wanted to know whether additional teachers would be placed in the room to take care of them so that their own "normal" children would not be shortchanged, they were told no.

What do you think? Was your initial reaction to the idea of having handicapped kids mingle with yours positive or negative? Did you feel that children in Washington School would be enriched watching their peers struggling against insurmountable handicaps to achieve, or were you concerned only for your own son or daughter?

The Disturbing Reality

The disturbing reality in America today is that most of our first reactions to the above situations are negative. For example, the history of opening group homes in this country has most often been met with bigotry, hostility, harassment, and lawsuits. Community after community has sought to block the establishment of group homes by way of the courts. And, sad to say, irate neighbors in some towns have burned down group

---

And Jesus said: "Foxes have holes and birds of the air have nests, but the Son of Man has nowhere to lay his head."   —*Matthew 8:20*

---

homes in a last-ditch effort to prevent their continuance. Others, more often than not, have been subject to picketing, brick throwing, and hurtful insults. Parents have admonished their children not to go near "those people."

In surveys, however, most community populations support the concept of community-based group homes—*but not in their neighborhood!* They are unaware that such homes are more efficiently run than the state institutions, hence a better return for their tax dollar. They don't stop to think of the advantages that the disabled enjoy in efficiently managed living environments that allow them some much-needed dignity, and they dismiss the argument that "these people" might benefit greatly from living in "good" neighborhoods.

In employment, even though the Civil Rights Act of 1975 guarantees free and equal employment opportunities, persons with disabilities in this country are still the largest unemployed minority. Recent surveys indicate that almost 60% of all disabled adults are unemployed, while even more live well below the nationally established poverty level. Being disabled in America means that a prospective employer recognizes the disability first—the ability second.

Despite the law of the land—the right to free and equal education—parents of disabled children must constantly fight the school systems to ensure that appropriate physical plant alterations make access possible for their offspring, both in and out of the classroom. Education for the disabled remains an expensive proposition, and in an era of diminishing federal funding, parents of "normal" and "gifted" children are asking

---

And Jesus said: "Whoever receives one child in my name receives me."   —*Matthew 18:5*

---

openly why their children may be slighted for the sake of children with disabilities. It seems that the "they-are-different" mentality prevails along with the battle-cry of maintaining the status quo.

Less than fifty years ago, Nazi Germany determined that its disabled citizens were really a drain on society and exterminated them along with the Jews. Now, in our own country, we are beginning to hear the catch phrase "quality of life," a phrase that no doubt began with the good intention of making us aware of our environment but has taken on overtones about how we make life-or-death decisions regarding, for example, who is worthy to receive certain welfare services. By extension, it is but a small step to determine who is to live in the sick wards and what infant who is born malformed should be given supportive systems to survive. In the long run such an attitude affects the way we value human beings. While our laws and sense of morality would militate against the steps the Nazis took, nevertheless, we must guard against the insidious and often unconscious practices we exhibit by committing thousands of the disabled to a form of psychological extermination by excluding them from the mainstream of American life.

Our challenge, then, as Christians, is to confront our prejudices, acknowledge them and make them our own, and root them out of our lives and communities, lest we continue to sin against justice. By doing so, our lives, our parishes, and our country will be richer. As Catholics, we must heed the words of the bishops in their statement on the handicapped: *. . . in order to be loyal to its calling, to be truly pastoral, the parish must make sure that it does not exclude any Catholic who wishes to take part in its activities.*

This, and only this, the Lord God asks of you: to act justly, to love tenderly, and to walk humbly with your God.   —*Micah 6:8*

4

To Be Disabled

Look for a moment at yourself: sound of mind, body, and spirit. Now suppose that you've been through a catastrophic illness or accident that has put you in a wheelchair for the rest of your life. Imagine doing the usual things: the daily activities of bathing, dressing, preparing meals, and putting the cat out. You'd probably need a lot of help, especially at first. Then you'd think of how you were going to negotiate shopping or attending church. What changes would you be forced to make? Who could you rely on for help, perhaps on a daily basis? Tough questions to have to face, but newly disabled persons must suddenly face them and come to terms with the different lifestyle that has been thrust upon them.

Coming to terms with oneself for people who all their lives have prided themselves on their health and independence can be extremely difficult. Some are so passive and depressed that they make no effort to ask for help. Others who know they must seek help have trouble asking for it. Still others look at what has befallen them as God's will, and sometimes a sense of punishment or shame comes over them, as happened in Mary's family in our case history.

You might discover that attending church becomes a low priority for you. You've been used to picking the Mass you

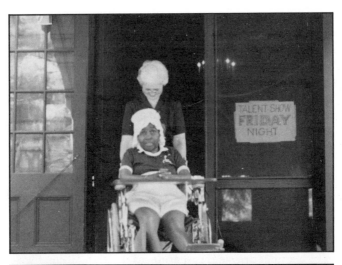

wanted to attend and then driving to the church. Now you must rely on someone else to get you there, and you'll feel compelled to go when that person deems it convenient. Freedom of choice becomes limited, and frustration that is dictated by your having to be dependent on others leads to a feeling of utter rejection and hopelessness.

Once in the church, they assign you a "place" that is reserved for wheelchairs. It's easy to feel different, now. You're in the area reserved for the handicapped, and you quickly learn

---

Do not fear those who deprive the body of life but cannot destroy the soul. . . . As for you, every hair of your head has been counted.
—*Matthew 10:28-30*

---

your new "place" in life. Could you possibly continue your job as lector? Would Father even consider asking? What's the sense? The whole congregation would stare at you.

And what about going to Communion? Can you get there yourself, or will you have to be wheeled up front later on, so as not to be a nuisance to the rest of the communicants? With things like this going on all the time now, you begin to question whether you've lost your humanity along with your mobility. It was so different before. You didn't have to wait, didn't have to rely on someone else. You always took care of yourself.

Mass is over, and you're wheeled out without having indicated that you wanted to leave just then. You think "Why didn't they at least ask me if I was ready? Can't people see that beyond my disability I am still a real person—with real feelings? If they would only see my humanity instead of just my calamity!" And so it goes—from now until the day that you die. Will you learn to live with it? If you were whole again, would you see the disabled in a new and different light? You know the answer.

> He went round the whole of Galilee teaching in their
> synagogues, proclaiming the good news of the king-
> dom and curing all kinds of disease and illness
> among the people.   —*Matthew 4:23*

Considering a Ministry

Now that you've considered what being disabled might mean
in the way of having to change the way you've always done
things, perhaps you're ready to consider what a ministry to
the handicapped might entail.

The task is clear: Jesus said, "Follow me," and the bishops'
statement explains that . . . *the central meaning of Jesus' ministry is bound up with the fact that he sought the company of
people who for one reason or another, were forced to live on
the fringe of society. . . . The Church finds its true identity
when it fully integrates itself with these "marginal
people". . . .*

Jesus healed people wherever he went. He prayed over
them, he touched them and was touched by them, these un-
clean and untouchable castoffs from society. He had compassion for them, and power went out from him. He made the
blind see and the deaf hear; he restored health to withered

> And Jesus said: "Come to me, all you who labor
> and are heavy laden, and I will give you rest."
>   —*Matthew 11:28*

limbs; he raised the dead—all to show that God had given him
power over life and death. Nowhere did he teach that sick-
ness came from God, or that suffering was inflicted as a test
to be endured. Those ideas come to us by way of two Latin
word roots that have colored our views of health and healing

for centuries. They are *salvo*, having to do with salvation from sin, and *sano*, having to do with health of the body. Somewhere in the early Church the two words became somewhat confused, and the idea grew that a disability was a manifestation of a person's sinfulness.

We can follow Jesus by caring for the disabled—caring about them and for them, touching them, listening to them, believing in them, seeing that their rights are given them. We can make a conscious Christian decision to embrace their needs and to become one with them as they try to secure for themselves equal employment, equal education, and above all, dignity as true human beings.

We can also help change others' attitudes toward the disabled. As we grow in compassion, we can mend hearts and heal misunderstandings. We can overpower the indifference and lack of compassion. We can destroy myths and make others see past wheelchairs into hearts and minds. This we can do to follow Jesus. And doing it will make us more human.

But a Samaritan, as he journeyed, came to where he was; and when he saw him, he had compassion, and went to him and bound up his wounds . . .
—*Luke 10:33-34*

A church entrance and interior with ideal flat-surface accessibility for persons with disabilities.

5

Getting Started in Ministry

Now that you are aware of what it means to be handicapped, what some of the laws are regarding disabled people, and exactly what Jesus' example may mean to you, perhaps you're wondering how to get started in your own ministry to persons with disabilities. This booklet assumes that your ministry will take root at the parish level, and that means, first of all, that you will share your knowledge and newly acquired gift of wanting to minister with other parish members, your family, and friends.

Before beginning, however, take the time to explore your own personal attitudes and feelings about the disabled. Spend some prayerful time to search them out, for it is your feelings that are the real you. By working through your own feelings,

---

The Church . . . must reach out to welcome gratefully those who seek to participate in the ecclesial community.
—*Pastoral Statement on the Handicapped*

---

you'll be better prepared to help those you hope to enlist in your ministry to become aware of the problems facing the disabled. As you make your fellow parishioners more aware of these problems, you'll no doubt see a change come over them as some of your zeal to follow Jesus' example rubs off on them. Together, then, your group can start to create a parish environment that will reach out to the disabled in such a way that the bishops' statement to the handicapped comes alive: *The Church . . . must reach out to welcome gratefully those who seek to participate in the ecclesial community.*

You should get your pastor involved, too. Remember, he has a captive audience at least once a week, and he will be able to help your ministry group to focus the entire parish's attention on the handicapped, perhaps using the bishops' pastoral statement as his point of departure. And there may be others on the parish staff or council whose talents would lend themselves to this ministry. Don't be afraid to ask for their assistance.

Next, you must identify those members (perhaps nonmembers, too) within parish boundaries who are disabled. Some of them you'll know from having seen them in church. There will be others who gave up struggling to get to Mass years ago. You will have to make a list of them, with their varying degrees of disability. Then you will have to assess each individual's personal needs. Are they crippled? Are they deaf? What can our parish do to make their visits to church comfortable, let alone possible?

A good start is to determine the scope of your ministry. That will depend on the size and population of your parish, but for now let's consider the needs for a medium-sized community.

You should form three committees: a Buildings and Grounds Committee, a Fellowship Committee, and a Service Committee. In this way, committee members can focus on specific issues, and this kind of focus tends to maximize a com-

Jesus entered a village, and a woman named Martha received him into her house.   —Luke 10:38

Each one of us, however, has been given a share
of grace, given as Christ allotted it.
                                        —*Ephesians 4:7*

mittee member's commitment. Make clear to each committee
just what its goals are, and just how it fits in with your overall
mission as spelled out in the bishops' statement to the handicapped.

The Building and Grounds Committee. This committee should
be made responsible for assessing the physical facilities of the
church, parish hall, parking area, school, and rectory. Ideally,
all of these facilities should have street-level entrances or a very
gradual, broad ramp. Entrances should allow a physically disabled person to enter buildings with the rest of the parish and
not be relegated to a "back door" entry. All main entrance areas
should have railings, so that persons with mobility problems
will have support on slick or icy days. Part of a pew, somewhere toward the front of the church, could be removed to
allow a person in a wheelchair to sit among the congregation
and participate in Communion comfortably. All doors should
be at least thirty-four inches wide, to allow a wheelchair easy
passage. Rest room doors should also be wide enough to allow wheelchairs to go through easily, and at least one com-
mode with a grab bar is essential for disabled elderly, as well
as wheelchair users.

Water fountains, public phones, light switches, door handles,
elevator buttons, and literature racks should be low enough
so that a person in a wheelchair can reach them. You might
sensitize the members of this committee to the typical needs
of a disabled person by having one or two members of the com-

And the blind and the lame came to him in the
temple, and he healed them.   —*Matthew 21:14*

mittee come to church in a wheelchair and spend the entire morning in the building, trying to participate in all of the morning's activities.

Be sensitive, also, to the needs of the blind. Braille editions of missalettes, hymnals, and other literature should be provided

---

Jesus said: "I am the light of the world."

—*John 8:12*

---

for parishioners who are blind. In addition, important signs, such as those for rest rooms, elevators, etc., should be rendered in braille, allowing a blind person the dignity of maximum independence. Your local office of the commission for the visually handicapped can suggest sources for braille services.

As the Buildings and Grounds Committee becomes more familiar with its task, it will undoubtedly discover other areas that can be improved: the height of curbs, removal of potted plants that are obstacles, and many more such things hitherto overlooked.

The Fellowship Committee. This committee is responsible for locating disabled parishioners and extending a welcome to them and their families. The initial contact should be kept primarily on a one-to-one basis, if possible, and a low-profile, low-keyed approach is best. The welcome, of course, must be warm and sincere and in the spirit of wanting to help. Committee members should be prepared to be rebuffed initially, as many families and disabled people are extremely sensitive about their condition. As a follow-up, the committee might write letters to these people, outlining the concern of the parish, suggesting physical improvements they might find more accommodating, and leaving the door open to them.

As the committee becomes more organized, it might plan two or three special activities that would be appropriate for certain groups of disabled people, such as the mentally retarded and their families. Members might also take on the pleasant responsibility of sending birthday cards or Christmas and Thanksgiving greetings. Another project would involve phoning people who are alone a great deal of the time, a kind of "just checking" program that is easy to do, yet means so much to a shut-in.

The Service Committee. This group must initiate special parish programs to handle the needs of the disabled and their families. It must learn, especially, to understand the feelings of isolation that such families often endure. Committee members will meet a wide range of emotional problems within these families: denial, hostility, rage, jealousy, overprotection—even martyrdom. The committee will have to explore ways to make these families whole again and bring them back to a healthy outlook with normal personal interaction. Given the dynamics, the first and most difficult task will be to win their trust and confidence.

The easiest way to promote trust and understanding is to establish some "safe" and intimate family settings that are conducive enough for them to open up a little about their fears and feelings of helplessness. Once they realize that you are

---

. . . injustices must be eliminated and ignorance and apathy replaced by increasing sensitivity and warm acceptance.
—*Pastoral Statement on the Handicapped*

---

genuinely concerned about them, that you're willing to listen to them and empathize with their plight, these burnt-out souls will gradually share their thoughts with you. Later on, they may even feel free enough to speak with larger discussion groups, perhaps even becoming future resource people that you can call upon to help others who come after them. But they will need a lot of time to come around. Once you get this far, your committee will have to determine just what specific help might be appropriate for the families, because it is usually at this point that such people become ready to accept what you are trying to offer them.

For example, you may be able to steer them to agencies whose sole purpose is to help the handicapped. Maybe they've never heard of the Department of Rehabilitative Services, called by different names in different states. This federally funded program assists newly disabled persons to live more independently and, if at all possible, to return to work. In addition, state and local mental health centers are found in many communities in the country today and can assist not only persons who have chronic mental illness but the newly mentally disabled who may be having adjustment problems.

You will find in most every state an agency for assisting the blind, where they'll introduce you to the Talking Book Program. These talking books are sent postage free to anyone with impaired vision, and the program even provides a cassette tape player, if necessary. There are similar offices for the hearing impaired.

If you have deaf people in your parish, it is very important that you obtain the services of an interpreter who is skilled in the art of signing. Your local speech or hearing center or office of vocational rehabilitation will be able to help you here. You should know, too, and be able to advise your deaf friends, that the courts have a legal obligation to provide signing interpreters for any deaf person who may have to appear in a law court, for whatever charge.

Newly injured persons are usually entitled to Social Security Disability Income (SSDI) that automatically entitles the person to medical and vocational services. SSDI is administered through the Social Security Administration and is authorized upon an individual's proving disability, a frequently dehumanizing process for which moral, if not legal, support may

Master, to whom shall we go? You alone have the
words of eternal life.   —John 6:68

be necessary to ensure that the proper benefits are forthcoming.

Don't leave a stone unturned. There are numerous federal, state, local, and private agencies that can be called upon to help. At last, public and private money is being channeled in the direction of the handicapped. Your Service Committee should maintain a list of all such services and make their existence known to all persons with disabilities.

Finally, the Service Committee can make certain that your people have transportation to the doctor, the grocery store, the Social Security Office, etc. The committee should also alert the Fellowship Committee about shut-ins who have no one to remember them on their birthdays or during the holidays. Very often community services can be enlisted to help out here. The possibilities of this and all other committees are limited only by the individual member's creativity, energy, and spiritual motivation.

Bridging the Gap

In your newfound ministry you might want to adopt the slogan "Bridging the Gap." As Christians, you know that persons with physical or mental limitations need to belong to the inclusive Church. By providing the necessary physical equipment, removing the barriers to make building access available to all, and planning creative programs, you can bridge that gap between a feeling of not belonging and belonging. By taking these first steps, you may also be providing an opportunity for some community problem-solving, always a positive way to make parishioners come closer together.

For example, one parish at first thought they needed to install an elevator to service the needs of some elderly folks, as well as those of disabled parishioners. The parish council appointed a committee to contact an architect and some contractors to study the feasibility and the cost. The committee came up with the staggering figure of $40,000, and that was the cost of the cheapest elevator!

At that point, several committee members began to investigate less expensive alternatives. They decided that a series of small ramps, wider stairs, and a mechanical stair-glide for the longest staircase would do the job. Volunteers offered to build the ramps, and a parishioner donated the lumber. The stair-glide would cost $8,000, so various committees set out to raise funds through the usual garage sales and bake sales, and a number of Church members made generous gifts. The money was raised in less than two weeks. Not only was the church made more accessible, but a large number of people had become involved in the project, and it made them feel good.

One important fringe benefit was that many had become truly sensitive to the needs of the physically disabled in the Church, and those with the disabilities felt as if their needs were really important to the entire parish. It was a beautiful and holy learning experience. It was a ministry group that had brought all this about—and had truly bridged the gap between people.

She heard about Jesus and came through the crowd
and touched his cloak.   —*Mark 5:27*

6

Advocacy and Resources

Becoming an Advocate

Becoming an advocate means becoming a listener. For only by listening to what is truly important to persons with disabilities can you become advocates for them. If you are able-bodied, your particular biases, likes, or dislikes are irrelevant if you truly want to become an advocate. You may want to change the world, but in reality a single curb lowered or removed, a crossing light, or a ride to the grocery store may be the most important thing to someone who is disabled in your parish. Find out what is needed by those in the parish and then try to tackle what is most important to them.

There is a constant need for legislative programs for the disabled. You can become an informed letter writer. The key word here is informed. That doesn't mean you have to be an expert. It does mean that you must do your homework and get your facts straight before you write. Check with a disabled person or a professional group if you are unsure of the facts. Make your letter simple. Explain your interest and support.

One of the most important services you can give disabled people is transportation. They need to have transportation to vital services: the doctor, the health department, the welfare office, Social Security Office, etc. They also should have transportation that allows them to go to the movies, the mall, the grocery store, and church without always having to inconvenience another person. Accessible public transportation for persons with disabilities is prohibitively expensive for many communities. However, with support from the federal government, many communities are now beginning to develop innovative and highly accessible transportation programs.

The Bay Area Rapid Transit system (BART) in San Francisco is reputedly one of the country's most effectively developed systems for the disabled. Transbuses, which have wheelchair capacity, are being used increasingly by large municipal transit systems in Philadelphia, Los Angeles, and Miami. As transbuses become more available, you might urge your community and local transportation officials to purchase them. They are available through Urban Mass Transit Authority (UMTA) funds.

Almost all disability groups throughout the country today need more money. Disability is a lifelong condition, and it requires a lifelong supply of money to deal with it. Disabled persons and programs that provide services for them are always looking for dollars to allow them to meet unmet needs, to start new programs, or just to survive. One tangible form of advocacy is to offer to help in one or more of the fund raising

---

. . . in order to be loyal to its calling, to be truly pastoral, the parish must make sure that it does not exclude any Catholic who wishes to take part in its activities.

—*Pastoral Statement on the Handicapped*

---

projects that recur each year. If you do offer, however, don't be surprised if you are greeted, initially, with suspicion. Directors and other professionals working with community pro-

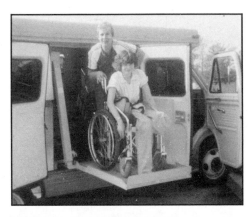

The lift mechanism in the van above provides mobility and transportation. The device attached to the car below lets handicapped drivers access their own wheelchairs.

grams are used to receiving so little support that they may wonder if you are really sincere. Show them that you are!

The clergy, religious, and laity engaged in this program should help the parish by developing policy and translating it into practical strategies for working with handicapped individuals.
—*Pastoral Statement on the Handicapped*

Some Resources to Get You Started

If your parish has never worked with disabled people, it is going to be important to locate resource people to assist you. They are all around you, and even the smallest communities will no doubt have some people who can assist your group.

A word of caution: Avoid the image of a "do good" group that gives the impression of wanting to help "those poor people" out of a sense of duty. Most professionals in the health care/rehabilitation field are already overworked and struggling with a tremendous amount of frustration. Most professionals will be more than happy to work with your group IF they feel your interest is genuine and sincerely motivated.

With those words of advice out of the way, where can you find resource people? The first step is to talk to some disabled people themselves. Some may be willing to share and others may not, but they are your best resource. They understand and know what their needs are. Do your best to listen if they express a willingness to work with you.

It is unlikely that all disability groups will be represented in your parish, so here is a list to help you locate professionals or helpful resources.

Advocacy Groups

The Association for Retarded Citizens
The Cerebral Palsy Association
Epilepsy Foundation
Groups for the Hearing Impaired and the Blind
Multiple Sclerosis Groups
Muscular Dystrophy Groups
Post-Polio Groups
Special Olympics
Mental Illness Groups

Professionals

Mental Health Centers
Workshops/Vocational Rehabilitation Programs
Adult Day-Care Programs
Easter Seal Societies
Rehabilitation Hospitals
Developmental Centers
School Systems
Department/Division of Mental Health
Department/Division of Mental Retardation
Developmental Disabilities Administration
Department/Division of Vocational Rehabilitation
Department for the Visually Impaired
Center for Hearing Impaired
Speech and Hearing Center
Physical Therapists
Occupational Therapists
Speech Therapists

Catholic Resources

The National Catholic Office serving persons with
disabilities is located in Washington, D.C., at 401

Michigan Ave. N.E. This office has a board of directors representing a broad spectrum of disabilities, persons on other national boards, and a number of bishops representing different geographic regions throughout the United States.

The office can also supply specific requests for equipment, up-to-date information on what is happening nationally to persons with disabilities, programs to help sensitize parishes to the needs of persons with disabilities, and resource people to assist you at the parish level.

Diocesan Offices are being established in every diocese to assist parishes with:

- Making our churches barrier free
- Ongoing spiritual development of persons with disabilities
- Assisting parish staff in meeting the different needs of persons with disabilities.

A Successful Ministry

Your desire to minister to persons with disabilities will be successful because of your prayers and your sincere attempt to reach out to ALL members of the parish. You will begin to live out the call of the American bishops in their statement on serving disabled persons: *The clergy, religious, and laity engaged in this program should help the parish by developing policy and translating it into practical strategies for working with handicapped individuals.*

With the help of this booklet, you can map out your own strategy to begin a ministry to the disabled. You can prevent what happened to Mary, the nonperson we discussed in the beginning chapter. Most of all, your ministry will make your parish community a good place for everyone.

Helpful Literature About the Disabled

Books

Hale, Gloria. *The Source Book for Disabled.* (An illustrated guide to easier and more independent living for physically disabled people, their family, and friends) Paddington Press, N.Y. 1979.

Katz, Alfred H. and Martin Knute. *A Handbook of Services for the Handicapped.* Westport, Conn. Greenwood Press, 1982.

Appendix I	Value-laden Beliefs and Principles for Rehabilitation listing
Appendix II	National Advocacy Consumer, and Voluntary Organizations listing
Appendix III	State Volunteer sponsored Information and Referral Services listing
Appendix IV	State Programs for Crippled Children, Developmental Disabled and Vocational Rehabilitation listing

Kern, Rev. Walter. *Pastoral Ministry with Disabled Persons.* Staten Island, N.Y. Alba House, 1985.

Kreisler, Jack and Betty. *Catalog of Aids.* (for organizations, agencies, and other sources of help) New York. McGraw-Hill, 1982.

Lunt, Suzaane. *A Handbook for the Disabled.* (ideas and inventions for easier living) New York. Scribner and Sons, 1982.

MacNutt, Francis. *The Power to Heal.* Notre Dame, Ind. Ave. Maria Press, 1977.

Mitchell, Joyce Slayton. *See Me More Clearly* (career and life planning for teens with physical disabilities) New York. Harcourt Brace, 1980.

Monty, Shirless. *Mays Boy*. Nashville, Tenn. Thomas Nelson,

Ohsberg, Oliver H. *The Church and Persons with Handicaps*, Scottdale, Penn. Herald Press, 1982.

Articles in Journals

Heller, E. B. "Cooperative Planning for the Paraplegic Veteran:" help from social agencies for those coming to Bulova School of Watchmaking. *Journal of Social Casework*, No. 29. (Feb. 1948) 66–69.

Holodnak, H. B. "Integration of Professional Services in the Rehabilitation of the Physically Handicapped." *Catholic Charities Review*, Vol. 31. (Feb. 1947) 35–38.

Switzer, M. E. "Preparation of the Sisterhood to Meet the Hospital Problems of the Future," *Hospital Progress*, Vol. XXV. No. 8 (Aug. 1944) 211–214.

Articles

Leonhardt, Thomas J., S.J. "Does Healing Bother you?" *Catholic Digest*. (April 1986) 65–69.

McBride, Alfred O. "The Church in the Year 2000," *St. Anthony Messenger*. (Feb. 1984) 29–31.

Booklets

Mortiz, Sister Mary. "The Handicapped: How to Show We Care," Albuquerque, N.M., Servant to the Faith Community.

Brief

Federal Emergency Management Agency. National Emergency Training Center, Emmitsburg, Md., Sept. 16, 1987.

Pastoral

National Conference of Catholic Bishops. U.S. Catholic Conference, 1312 Massachusetts Ave. N.W., Washington, D.C. 20005-4105. *Pastoral Statement on Handicapped People.* 1978.

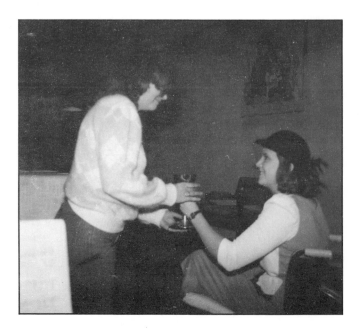

Two ways to allow easy access to church buildings: top photo shows electric lift to upper level; ramp at bottom is economical and easy to build.

Building Checklist

Type of Building

____Mobile unit
____Sub-basement
____One-story
____Split level
____Two story
____Round

Building Entrance

Number of steps____
Ramp? Yes____No____
Railings? Yes____No____
Flat (no steps)? Yes____No____

Doors

Outside doors open: Out____In____
Door opening width: 24"____36"____
Doors open easy with one hand? Yes____No____
How many doors to go through before getting to pews?____

Inside the Church

Aisle width? 3'____5'____6'____
Steps? Yes____No____
Altar visible from any seat? Yes____No____
Area for wheelchairs? Yes____No____
  Where? Side____Up front____Among worshipers____
  Other places____

Fire Exits
  Fire doors? Yes____No____
  Fire door width: 24"____36"____
  Illuminated exit signs? Yes____No____

Diagram for exiting? Yes____No____
Firefighting equipment? Yes____No____Kind:_____

Meeting Rooms (cry rooms, parish hall, classrooms, cafeteria, confessional)

Steps? Yes____No____Where?_____
Are meeting rooms in different buildings? Yes____No____
Ramps? Yes____No____
Elevators? Yes____No____
Flat surfaces throughout? Yes____No____

Floor Coverings

____Carpet
____Wood
____Vinyl
____Rough
____Slippery

Choir

Steps? Yes____No____
Ramp? Yes____No____
Flat surface? Yes____No____
Location: Front of church?____
        Back of church?____
            Upstairs?____ Can wheelchair person get
            upstairs? Yes____No____

Bathrooms

Steps? Yes____No____
Flat? Yes____No____
Doors swing: In____Out____
Door width____
Wheelchair access to toilet stall (private)? Yes____No____
Wheelchair access close to toilet itself for easy transfer?
        Yes____No____
Grab bars? Yes____No____

Tissue/towels low enough to reach from wheelchair?
Yes____No____
Approach to lavatory sink is clear? Yes____No____;
Sink low enough? Yes____No____

Altar
Steps? Yes____No____
Lectern height: 3'____5'____
Can wheelchair person minister at/from the altar?
Yes____No____

Assisting Devices
Braille signs? Yes____No____
Hearing aids? Yes____No____(confessional)
Public phones three feet from floor? Yes____No____
Coat rack three feet from floor? Yes____No____
Elevator? Yes____No____
Ramps? Yes____No____
Large print missalettes? Yes____No____
Braille missalettes/hymnals? Yes____No____

Parking Facilities

Parking lot? Yes____No____
Street parking? Yes____No____
Curb cuts (wheelchair access)? Yes____No____
Reserved places for handicapped? Yes____No____
How many?
Personal assistance for wheelchair persons to and from lot?
Yes____No____